Don't Waste Your Vapor
Alvin Rucker

Don't Waste Your Vapor
Alvin Rucker

© 2017 Alvin Rucker
Don't Waste Your Vapor

Cover photo by Harrod Publishing
Edited by Michelle Yates, IWriteIEditIProofread

All rights reserved. No part of this publication may be reproduced, stored in a retrieval system, or transmitted in any form or by any means -- electronic, mechanical, photocopying, recording, or otherwise -- without the prior written permission of author or publisher.

Published by Harrod Publishing
www.harrodpublishing.com
harrodpublishing@gmail.com
(240) 244-6082

Author's Contact: *akrucker@bellsouth.net*

Printed in the United States
Library of Congress
Harrod Enterprises LLC

Don't Wate Your Vapor
Alvin Rucker

ISBN: 978-0-9960763-1-9

Dedication and Acknowledgements

I thank and praise God for all He has done and is doing in my life. I give honor to Jesus Christ my champion and Savior! He is indeed the reason I have a mind to serve in the Kingdom of God. I must begin by thanking my lovely wife, Kelli L. Rucker, for being my greatest cheerleader, supporter and best friend for the past 27 years we have been together. I thank God for my one and only son, Dylan "Hercules" Charles Rucker! You are my inspiration, and you drive me to excellence!

I dedicate this book to my dear grandmother, the late Mrs. Ollie Mae Hunt. She spoke into my life so many times as we sat and talked for hours and hours. She shaped my character!

To my namesake and my grandfather, the late Deacon Alvin Hunt, I say thank you for instilling in me Godly character. You always took time to show me things, even when I was disturbing your work.

I also dedicate this book to my mother, Mrs. Carolyn Rucker, and my father, the late Mr. Mack Rucker. You two raised me to be a God-fearing man, and I appreciate all of the love and support.

I also dedicate this work to my awesome sister, Mrs. Karen Yvette Huling, and my cool little brother, Barnard Rucker. You two are the best siblings in the world. I love you! I would love to list all of other family members, but I would run out of ink…LOL! You all had and still have space in my heart!

To my spiritual parents, the late Bishop M.J. Pace III, and Bishop Liza Hickman. You two are the reason for my spiritual foundation. My wife and I so appreciate your anointed guidance, selfless service and love during our young adult years! We are family for LIFE!

To the countless spiritual brothers and sisters in the Lord, I salute you!

Last but not least, I dedicate this book to my church family, *One Accord Family Ministries*. You are second to none. You guys are the reason I push so hard toward that mark!!! This is just the beginning of great things to come!

Pastor Alvin M. Rucker

Introduction

The Bible states in James 4:14 (NKJV); *"whereas you do not know what will happen tomorrow. For what is your life? It is even a vapor that appears for a little time and then vanishes away."*

It is interesting that the Word of God compares precious life to that of a mere *vapor*. It is interesting to think of life being something as simple as a gaseous form of substance, which screams vulnerability and a very fragile state of being. This notion alone should cause us to treasure our lives and every moment regardless if these moments are good, bad or indifferent. Why do we tend to focus so much energy on creating that big, earth-shaking event that will cause an intoxicating feeling of purpose? Is that the whole point of this *vapor* we are given? In this book, we will explore some areas of our lives in an attempt to answer some of these questions.

As a believer in Jesus Christ, we know that the Word of God is our road map of life. It is my prayer that this book will be a tool that will enhance your spiritual walk, and point you back to your relationship with the Father. This life we are given is so precious that words cannot capture its significance. There's an adage that I love to quote that says, "We only have one life to live." This is so true. We should not get to the end of our lives and allow regret to dominate our last ounces of *"vapor!"* We must strive to appreciate this precious gift of life and embrace each moment with totality.

Chapter 1

Embracing Your NOW!

We live in a society that teaches us to dig deep within ourselves and maximize our potential. The goal has become to become number one, compete with and dominate the best and possess the most power, popularity, and pennies (money). I would like to challenge this type of thinking because it is not the mindset or goal that Father God intended for His people to possess. If not careful, we can miss or misappropriate Godly energy by concentrating on the future while negating to appreciate the now. Be careful not to miss the blessing of this moment while living in the uncertainty of the next.

Why do we need to embrace need we embrace our NOW? What exactly does this mean? I am so glad you asked. I'd like to begin the response to this question with Hebrews 11:1, which declares, "Now faith is the substance of things hoped for, the evidence of things not seen." The real focus of this verse is NOW. The Word now causes one to move at that moment. While planning for tomorrow is a good thing we must also be cognizant of must also know of the fact that not even the next minute is promised.

It seems as if the thought of most of the humanity is geared toward doing better when one obtains a certain amount of money, status or position. However, those same things you see yourself doing then could be achieved right now! I honestly believe this is the reason God called it now faith and not later faith. For example, my now faith is compelling me to pen this book and not to wait until I have proverbially "arrived" before I start moving move toward my God-given destiny.

Vapor: noun - a visible exhalation, as fog, mist, steam, smoke, or noxious gas, diffused through or suspended in the air

Another aspect of embracing your now involves slowing down to listen and experience the given moment. I have found this exercise to be fulfilling. Here is an example of what I am talking about: It is 5:30 pm. My wife Kelli and my son Dylan sat down to eat dinner. I am in the kitchen fixing my plate. Before I walk into the dining room, I pause to listen to my surroundings. I may hear a car go down the street or hear someone cutting the grass. I then listen to what my son may be sharing with his mother about his day or what my wife is saying to our son. Within this pause, I can pick out so many blessings – we have a safe home, we live in a great neighborhood that is so peaceful, our family is unified, and love is present within our home. My son is a teenager and he still genuinely wants to engage in real conversation with his parents. All of this is realized within a matter of seconds.

Therefore, in that brief embracing of a NOW moment, my terrible day at work becomes minimized. The thought of life issues is now easier to handle because of this moment, which could easily be missed! Even as you are reading this book, this very moment is enhanced because you are reminded to embrace it. Your attitude may have been compromised due to bad experiences; however, you can evaluate the situation from the standpoint of Godly purpose and not from a mindset filled with a wounded ego or within a roller coaster of emotions.

I am about to make a distinct statement. The things we do now will positively or negatively affect us later. Would you agree with that? Ok, so the natural progression of thought after that would be, what state of mind do I need to act upon my NOW moment positively? The Bible declares in Philippians 2:4-5, "Look not every man on his own things, but every man also on the things of others. Let this mind be in you, which was also in Christ Jesus." We MUST possess the mind of Jesus Christ. In this passage, Jesus focused on others and not on Himself. When our Godly purpose is at the forefront, the cloud that seeks to hinder the "now" embrace will soon fade. With the right mindset, the fear, doubt and hurt that clouds the moment will begin to lose power. These attributes sent by the enemy of our souls (the devil) are merely momentary robbers. For example, if fear can convince us to sit on a God-given idea for an extended period, someone will have missed their moment of benefiting from that song, book, poem, blog or spoken word. We allow the fear factor to plant seeds of doubt to smother the dream/vision when we fail to embrace the moment.

Beloved, do not waste your *vapor* because it is more precious than you realize.

Let's go a bit deeper about momentary robbers. These events tend to act as extreme mind altering occurrences. To better illustrate this, let's take a standard issue that usually affects us all.

Relationships! At some point in our lives, we will all experience a relationship issue. It does not matter if your child is disobedient, a spouse is unbearable, or your sibling has joined a weird social group and no longer talks to you; the variable that is most important is not the issue, it is the response!

When we choose to focus primarily on the issue and how it has made us feel, we have already been robbed. No clear resolution can be birthed out of a response that is filled with emotion.

Let's take the first example of a disobedient child. We will explore the wrong way to go about things and a better way to handle the situation at hand.

Parent: Son, take out the garbage before you go play.
Child: Ahhh mom, can't somebody else do it?
Parent: No I asked you!

Child: Ok, I will – child ignores the chore and goes outside without taking out the trash!

The wrong *"vapor stealing"* response: "Why does this child continue to ignore me? I am getting so furious with this boy! This hurts me so much, and I bet he doesn't care!"

Better response: "I need to sit him down to discuss why he seems to be ignoring me. He was raised to obey his parents, and I know he is a good child. Jesus, please give me the words to say and the knowledge on how to handle this matter.

Believe it or not, one wrong response can spill over into other moments and before long soon that one occurrence has spread like a cancer that seeks to choke out every single minute assigned to your day! The turning point begins when one realizes that something is going wrong. It is here when one must take the time to get to the root of the issue without focusing on the flow of emotions.

Another way that we can embrace our now moment is by seeing the spiritual reward before it manifest. This is a trait of a visionary. The Bible teaches us to write the vision and makes it understandable. We would have to have a spiritual insight on said vision on the vision before we can write.

Writing the vision is an act of faith. The reason I believe that is because I believe that because we are creative beings designed by God, THE Creator. It is because of this that we can access the spiritual through dreams and visions. The difference between a visionary and a person that has a vision is that one that applies faith and writes it down with the intent to carry out the plan.

Once we see the plan (with our natural eye) it becomes even more tangible and obtainable.

This sighting can fuel the proverbial gift of HARD WORK! At this point, we must be careful than have to be careful not to allow doubt to talk to us. Doubt loves to start the comparison game within us. Doubt says He would say, "What are you doing? Are you not qualified to do this? What if people don't receive it?" You know honestly, When doubt begins to speak, we must ignore it doubt and believe that what we are doing is worthwhile. Just because the enemy of our souls does not want us to carry out the vision does not and should not stop us. Take a stable and sober posture to pursue.

When we begin to seize the moment, hard work begins to destroy slothfulness and procrastination! Hard work breeds a manifestation of Godly results. I am a firm believer that when we see good results, we tend to strive for more. Let us not become so complacent in victory lest we shall slip back into slothful stagnation. Let us not allow the moment of conquest to become a crutch when it's been assigned to catapult us into continuous conquests. Please, people, be mindful of this subtle occurrence.

Chapter 2

The Art of Acknowledging God

In this chapter, we are going to explore the necessity of acknowledging God the Father concerning about every aspect of our lives and being. The Word of God declares in Proverbs 3:6, "In all your ways acknowledge Him, and He shall direct your paths."

Too often we look at our daily path, and because we are familiar with the pattern of the day, we tend to skip over the acknowledgment. When we do that, we are telling God, "I got this one! I'll consult You when I get in trouble or confused."

So, it would seem like the only time we acknowledge God is when we are in trouble, or the familiar path has become a bit difficult. This is NOT recognizing and acknowledging God in ALL of our ways. We must shift our thinking when it comes to acknowledgment with acknowledgment. First, we have to realize that we NEED God to guide us. When we start to feel or act feel or act like we do not need to acknowledge God, we allow some hindrances to interfere with our relationship with God, the Father.

A massive hindrance to our acknowledgment is pride. The spirit of pride will always cause us to go against our spiritual conviction to just ask God. Pride is a cunning spirit that suggests to us a pseudo (false) confidence to rely on ourselves instead of God. As we know, our enemy, satan is a liar. He uses the spirit of pride to tell us half-truths.

Here is an example:

Pride: "You know God has matured you so much over the years. God doesn't want to hear about every detail of your life."

Our human response: "Well, God has indeed allowed me to grow, and I don't need to pray about everything because I pretty much know how most situations will go".

Our response is walking in the Spirit: "I am mature in the Lord, but I am still a servant of the Lord. Jesus sent us the Holy Spirit to guide us in all things, and the Word says that men should ALWAYS pray. I bind this spirit of pride that is trying to lead me away from acknowledging the Father!"

When we learn how to ask God about everything, even in the small things, we develop great attributes to our character, as well as and a keen ear to hear God's voice. Talking to God about it also sharpens our gift of discernment. The more we talk to God, the easier it becomes to recognize His voice. God's voice and instructions will always (I MEAN ALWAYS) line up with the Word of God. Sometimes the answer to our prayers is staring us right in our faces.

God can use everyday circumstances to show us His will.

Here is what I mean. Let's say you are riding down the street on your way home from the grocery store. You see an older lady walking in the rain. You and your family discuss, rather quickly, if you should give her for a ride. Now, it would seem that this is a no-brainer, right?. Of course, you should give her a ride, you're asking yourself. This situation will still require an acknowledgment from the Lord.

Ok, you seek the Lord quickly, and you are led by the peace of God to inquire if she needed a ride. She enters the vehicle, and she is incredibly thankful for the lift. She mentions that she had recently had surgery on her foot and the ride home was welcomed. This is not just an example; it happened to my family. Who knows what would have happened to this lady, if we had ignored the opportunity to assist her and gone straight home. Selah.

Another indicator in our lives that illustrates that we have negated to acknowledge God is the presence of frustration. I liken the emotion of frustration to that of lava in a volcano. It looks ok from the outside, but when you get closer to it, you can hear rumbling as the heat is rising from it. While it may not erupt that moment, if you give it time...it has the potential to boil over and alter or destroy everything it reaches. Therefore, if we allow frustration to hang around, we can be profoundly affected by this crafty emotion. The feeling of frustration can become like cancer and begin to regulate how we think, act and speak. You may be asking yourself why the Word of God urges us to be angry but sin not. Please understand that there is a glaring difference between anger and frustration. Anger is indeed a emotion that can become very heated. However, it is usually expressed verbally or physically before subsiding.

Frustration tends to linger lingers within a person and tries to search for ways to obtain control of a situation, another person or even God. Again, like cancer, these frustrating emotions will also circumvent Godly principals. When we feel this strange emotion, we need to we must IMMEDIATELY acknowledge God and ask for this to be removed out of us all.

Chapter 3

Turning Trials into Opportunities

The Word of God states, "In this life, you will have trials and tribulations but fear not, I have overcome the world." Problems, trials, issues and unfortunate circumstances are never fun to deal with. We never want to talk about things like this. Honestly, I don't either. However, the Word of God promises us that we will have them. That being said, however, let's explore some things that we can do to make these unfortunate circumstances work FOR us.

Romans 8:28 states, "All things work together for the good of them who are the called according to His purpose." That acknowledgment alone should help us process challenging times and awkward moments. This promise also gives us a lighter perspective on a matter.

Even when dealing with hurt, pain, and disgust; we can remind ourselves that at the end of the day God can use this issue to work in my favor.

An example of a trial:

A man (a believer in Jesus Christ) has just lost his job. Along with this catastrophe, he and his wife are at odds and are not getting along. The night before, she threatens to pack her bags and leave him if things did not get better for them. This man is now driving home after just being fired. He is hurt, angry and in shock of losing his job. He loves his wife dearly, and he knows that this news has the potential to cause more problems within the family. What does he do? How could this EVER work for the good?

A knee-jerk (fleshly) response: The man decides to get gets some flowers and dinner to take home to his wife. The couple enjoys dinner, and the mood of the home is right. To keep the peace in his marriage and home, he decides not to tell her about the job, gets up the next day, gets ready for work and drives around all day. He does this for several days and forgets that Friday has come and gone. Without fail, his wife expects a paycheck. He has now caused ANOTHER issue of mistrust and lies by trying to smooth things over. Now, this matter is not beyond repair, but it could have been an opportunity for healing if this man took another path.

A spiritually mature response: The man calls his wife immediately after he was fired and tells her he is on the way home and they need to they must discuss this right now. He is shaken and his voice trembles. His loving wife was angry about it but has compassion for him and agreed to hash everything out. Not only did they come, they came up with a financial plan (through prayer), but they discuss other issues that were bothering each of them. A lot of angry words came out, and very uncomfortable truths came to the surface during this discussion; however, reconciliation and understanding was the result. Did he still get fired? Yes! Were there anger issues to be sorted out? Yes! Nevertheless, there was no room for God to intervene through the power of AGREEMENT!

This husband and wife team begins to work within the church. Cleaning the church, working in the nursery and singing on the praise team were their favorite acts of service.

The Lord provided through these assignments. Fast forward five years, this couple relocated to her hometown and now are pastors of a church the Lord birthed out of these trials and many tests of life. I left a lot of details out of this scenario because one day my wife and I will tell the entire story in another book. Yes this situation happened to me and my beautiful wife of now 22 years. God is so good, and His Word is so true. He can make ALL.

THINGS work for the good!

People, when we are in the midst of an issue, we must allow truth to be the driver. We can't fool ourselves or anyone else involved. Covering up and telling lies will ALWAYS cause the circumstance to worsen. We must acknowledge God…ahhh, there's that acknowledgment factor again! It is so necessary though, when we face our giants, we need the Spirit of God (the Holy Spirit) to guide us through every step of the way.

Once we have our perspective together and we ask the Holy Spirit for guidance, it is time to listen. God's instructions will lead the way through this matter every time. If you take the time to track it (after you have come through it), you will probably find that the trial was necessary.

Have you ever been driving somewhere (in a hurry) and realize you forgot something? When you get back home, you realized that you left the stove on or a candlelit? It was a good thing you forgot something, huh? We never know do we? The very thing we see (at face value) as a problem or trouble could be the thing that keeps could keep us from destruction. We TRUST THE PROCESS! God knows the plans for our life. Ask for directions and stop thinking you know best. TRUST HIS PROCESS…TRUST GOD'S WORD!

Sometimes a trial or a suspicious circumstance comes into our lives to push slothfulness and laziness out of us. Does this type of push this pushes feel good? NO! Not! In most cases, usually it is necessary to embrace the push or nudge to do better. Too often our human nature will do just about anything to avoid uncomfortable circumstances. A comfortable place can sometimes produce the fruit of contentment and stagnation.

Therefore, a Godly perspective is paramount when discerning a trial. Most of the time our initial emotional response may be the wrong response for that moment. As we matriculate through life, we must take the time to pray before reacting to anything.

I know what you may be thinking about all this trial talk. Some may even question why the Bible promises trials in the life of the believer. The real question concerning about tests is not why, but how! How does this trial or circumstance fit into my journey? When we continuously ask the question of why we are WASTING VAPOR!! We must always take the posture of how and not why! Think about this, when we ask how we make a stance of action. How do we handle this? How do I manage as I go through this? On the other hand, when we ask how, we are taking a stance of fear? Why am I going through this? Why does everything have to be so hard? Do you see the difference? The question why sets us up to be defeated. But we thank God for grace and mercy that will cover us when we are taking a "why" stance! Our prayer should be, "Lord, please turn my why attitude into a "how" attitude!

Chapter 4

Now Faith vs. Desperation Faith

There is a definite difference between acting/moving in faith and acting/moving in desperation. I would like to start this chapter by defining each one.

Faith is defined as complete trust or confidence in someone or something (we are going to insert Father God here). Desperation is described as a state of despair, typically one that results in a rash or extreme behavior. That is a bit eye-opening, isn't it? One would think that these two types of faith that these two beliefs are one in the same. As we can see from the definition of desperation, there are glaring differences! If you have been a Christian for more than two over two minutes, you have heard the term, "Lord, I am desperate for You!" We will discover that this out of the garbage or even killing never enter this person's mind. The goal of eating trumps everything. They have a desperate faith that tells them "by any means necessary" get some food and get it now! I want to say that there is one prominent character trait here in this scenario that is a good one – *determination*!

Faith is a necessary and a consistent element of a spiritual existence. The Word of God states in Hebrews 11:1, "Faith is the substance of things hoped for…" So, our faith is made up of comprises something. What we are hoping for formulates a measure of confidence coupled with faith. A desperate form of hoping tends to taint our faith. Irrational or erratic behavior, even if done with great determination, can be more harmful to us that if we did nothing at all.

I want to illustrate this factor with the use of an athlete, let's say a basketball player. Young Billy Johnson has all the talent in the world! He is so good, and he has colleges looking at him while he's in the ninth grade. He is 6'8" already, and his skill set is beyond his years. He wakes up in the morning and plays ball before the sun rises. Fast forward to his college career, and he is impressive on the court his very first year. All his focus is on basketball. He no longer goes to class and is waiting to end the year so he can enter the NBA. Now, let's pause for a second. You can apparently see the glaring mistake he is making. Although his talent has the potential of making him rich and famous, he is not thinking about his personal and physical development. He is also throwing away the ability to obtain a college degree in which he could benefit from after basketball. His total faith (desperate faith) is solely in his ability. *Back to the example*: Billy and his team are in the final four tournaments, and Billy is playing like M.J. (Michael Jordan for those non-basketball fans). He helps his team win the tournament and declares for the NBA one day after the season ends. During the rookie workouts, Billy has a horrible knee injury that is so bad that it ends his playing days. Billy is now at home, no chance of going back to school on a scholarship, no job and he had no skills because he put all his faith into playing basketball. Now can Billy bounce back and have a productive life? Of course, He can. However, his choices would have been more excellent if he would have consulted God.

    This kind of blind, loose cannon faith is used way too often in our lives. There is nothing wrong with having a passion for something. It all must be balanced and within the framework of the God-given purpose of one's life. Billy would have been best to consult with his coaches, parents and or spiritual leaders concerning about his future endeavors. That is assuming those people mentioned would also have a Godly mentality themselves. Unfortunately, people have the same like-minded individuals around them that possess the same unstable characteristics.

We have talked about and illustrated on how not to believe. Now let us examine further a stable type of *Now Faith* – Hebrews 11:11 *"Now faith is the substance of things hoped for, the evidence of things not seen.* I believe a healthy faith is one that is built. It grows throughout a believer's life. One apparent way faith grows through experiencing great moments or answered prayer. Having an active faith at that time makes our confidence easy. I also want to state that a healthy level of faith can grow even during our most challenging moments. That does not sound quite right does it? How can my faith expand in a moment of sorrow, loss, calamity, destruction, etc.? How can my level of hope be strengthened during moments like these? Well, I am glad you asked those questions. Deriving from my personal experiences and my knowledge of the Word of God, faith picks up proverbial steam during challenges. Look at our brother Job in the Bible. God allowed the enemy to strip him of everything (even his good health). During the worst moments, he stated the following stated: "Though he (the devil) slay me, yet will I trust Him (God)." I tend to believe that Job's faith in God was strengthened merely because the devastation of his life that allowed him to realize what was most important…GOD! A tough spot has a way of working out of us what's in us *our real selves*. If we stop at the moment (not focusing on the circumstance) and allow the moment to teach us, we can grow from it. We can obtain strength to endure the next challenging moment. We learn that the last "punch" did not knock me out. I know that my God can and will see me through again!

A good measure of much of now faith also yields productivity. There is a chief robber of time called procrastination. His primary job is not to kill our joy, peace or the dreams. Procrastination is preferable, after the fire and energy of your dreams/visions/ideas. Has God given you something to do lately, an idea? You know it was God, now you are trapped between the idea and acting upon it. The passion and excitement are still there, but it fades ever so slightly as days become weeks – weeks become months – and so on! Faith without action is like a pot of gumbo with all the right ingredients that have no heat under it. The potential of it is very delicious. However, it will spoil and rot without the execution of cooking. SELAH!

As you can see, now faith is more efficient and edifying than desperate faith. When we operate in our now, we tend to alleviate the pitfalls of an emotional roller coaster. The ups and downs and turnarounds will make one spiritually unbalanced and unable to move forward. Even in the natural, when a person gets on a roller coaster, the experience of the dips and turns will cause them to become disoriented. Even when the ride is over, the uneasy motion still feels like it is happening. The person will have to person must take a moment to gather themselves before proceeding. The Bible teaches us that a double-minded man is unstable in all of his ways. Therefore, the goal is to be stable in ALL OF OUR WAYS! It is time to get away from operating within a "roller coaster" faith and embrace a stable "now" faith.

Chapter 5

God's Perfect Will

Have you ever heard the prayer, "Lord let Your will be done on earth as it is in heaven?" Sounds very familiar, doesn't it? Yes, it is in the Word of God:

> *Matthew 6:9-13(MSG)*

The world is full of so-called prayer warriors who are prayer-ignorant. They're full of formulas and programs and advice, peddling techniques for getting what you want from God. Don't fall for that nonsense. This is your Father you are dealing with, and he knows better than you what you need. With a God like this loving you, you can pray very simply. Like this:

> *Our Father in heaven,*
> *Reveal who you are.*
> *Set the world right;*
> *Do what's best - as above, so below.*
> *Keep us alive with three square meals.*
> *Keep us forgiven with you and forgiving others.*
> *Keep us safe from ourselves and the Devil.*
> *You're in charge!*
> *You can do anything you want!*
> *You're ablaze in beauty!*
>   *Yes. Yes. Yes.*

I wonder if we really know what we are praying when we declare His Word? Do we really want His will to be done in our lives? Do we know what His will is? In this chapter, we are going to dive into the real and tangible (yet practical) knowledge of the perfect will of God.

Romans 12:2 declares – *"Do not be conformed to this world, but be transformed by the renewal of your mind, that by testing you may discern what is the will of God, what is good and acceptable and perfect."*

Please underline perfectly in this passage because it is the goal of knowing God's will. One obvious factor here that should jump toward you is the fact that we cannot obtain or know God's will within the framework of a worldly mindset. God's perfect will always go against the norm. His perfect will is never rational. His perfect will tends to be is less obvious. We see throughout the Bible examples of impossible situations bringing God's Will to pass. The cross that Jesus Christ Himself had to bear is still the most UNLIKELY path to victory the earth has ever experienced! Jesus was falsely accused; everything would seem to be going seem to go against Him. He even asks God (His Father) to take away the task because it was so hard. However, something within Him (The Holy Spirit) let Him know to press on despite the hardship.

God's will never seem to feel good at the moment. Just like anything that is worth obtaining. It usually takes hard work to achieve it. As the old saying goes, if it were easy everybody would be doing it. The perfect will for our lives has a blueprint. Our God has the only copy, and we MUST obey His commands to carry it out!

Knowing God's will and doing the things He has commanded are two different things. The gap between hearing His perfect instructions and carrying them out is where victory resides. I honestly believe the hardest task is genuinely knowing the absolute will for our lives. A lot of us "waste *vapor*" when we spin our wheels on trying to figure out the perfect will.

I believe there are some great habits we can develop in our lives that will cause us to keep an open ear to His will. We should have and exercise a healthy prayer life. This is not merely saying a few words to God and barking out a few wants and needs to Him. Oh yeah, I might add for a mere five minutes before going to bed. A real prayer life consists of communing with God through a given day (every day).

When we do this, we develop an ear to know His voice. It becomes hard for the enemy to trip us up with his false instructions masking to be God.

We also learn of His will by knowing the Word of God. How do we learn things? I am glad you asked. We learn by reading, seeing and hearing. If you want to know the voice of God, you must know His Word! God never speaks outside of the framework of His Word (The Bible). Now please understand what I am saying. God does not speak to us with THUS, THOU and HINCE UNTOs. He speaks to us in our current vernacular. However, it will line up with His Word.

So, people of God, we cannot waste time with trying to develop a shortcut to obtaining our purpose. Father God is the King, and He holds the plans of our lives, Jeremiah 29:10-11(MSG) *"This is GOD's Word on the subject: "As soon as Babylon's seventy years are up and not a day before, I'll show up and take care of you as I promised and bring you back home. I know what I'm doing. I have it all planned out—plans to take care of you, not abandon you, plans to give you the future you hope for."* Trust the process and follow His leading. God loves us too much to lead us wrong. Only the enemy of our souls (the devil) wants to kick us off track. Focus on the process and not the problems and trials.

Chapter 6

Daily Reflection/Personal Accountability

It's 6 AM, and it is time to get up to start the day. The music is playing, and the television is still on from the night before. I hear the dog barking because he is ready for some food. Well, let me hit the snooze button because I have ten more minutes to sleep because I ironed my clothes last night. Wow, why does this bed feel so good right before I need to I must get up? Buzz, buzz…. ok, I guess I'll get up! It is 7:30 AM now, and we are all off to start the day. The children are being dropped off at school, my wife is on her way to work, and I am almost there. Let me turn on the radio to get my daily entertainment from my favorite morning radio personalities. I bet they have some good gossip for me! It is now 3:30 PM…wow will 5 PM ever get here? I need to, I must make it home because my wife is cooking my favorite meal and then we all will watch something funny on TV and go to bed. It is 10 PM now. I guess I will try. I will probably say something to God like now, for real??!! So, you want to talk to God now? I wonder how many moments have been squandered by sleeping that extra 10 minutes? If only you had been open to prayer.

I took you through that scenario to sort of put the mirror in front of us all. I am not saying we all do this, but I will bet that a lot of us do. I know that I have had "numb" days like this and then wonder why things in my life are not improving. This leads to taking frustrations out on everyone else (even God) when we should blame the person staring back at us in the mirror. We waste so many moments, opportunities and even trials by not taking the proper daily assessment.

I believe we should start our day off with moments of meditation, prayer and reading the Word. Even if you don't crack open a physical bible, speak the Word aloud shortly after waking up. I would challenge you to try this for a week to see how much better your day goes. Even amid tough times, when we do this our perspective will be much more balanced because we are not tackling things alone.

I recently took a personal account of my behavior. I noticed that I was doing the same things every day but expecting greater/better results. I believe that is called insanity, right? We must do better and better will follow. I would like to be transparent about a portion of my life right now. I am overweight, and I battle with eating sweets. I heard myself say to myself that I deserve a Snickers because I had a terrible day. Then the Spirit of God sheds the light on this lie. My flesh was telling me that fat and sugar was a treat. I don't know about you, but when I hear the word treat, it should mean something that is good for us. While a Snickers bar might taste good, it is far from a treat. A glass of water or a piece of fruit is a real treat. This spiritual reflection is helping me make some life-altering changes.

Ok, I hope that will help someone examine their lives a little closer. We should do daily reflections throughout the day, not just at the end of the day just. We should always be evaluating our actions and filtering them through the Spirit of God. I would dare say that a personal reflection might cause you to change a circumstance on the spot. What do I mean by that? Ok, here is what I mean. Let's say you are physically sick and someone comes up to you and says, "How are you doing?" You respond negatively and say, "I feel so bad, and I always get sick!" Yes, you ARE currently sick but to declare and agree that you ALWAYS get sick is not the will of God. Here is what you will say after you realize that statement was not a good one. You say, "Wait a minute, I am not always sick, and I should not say that. I might be feeling a bit under the weather now, but I know my God will heal me. Right now, I declare that I am healed now, in Jesus name!"

After we begin to develop this excellent habit of reflection, we can then couple it with personal accountability. I know you might be thinking that we should have accountability outside of ourselves (and we should). However, we should be accountable within and to ourselves as well ourselves. Personal accountability is not geared to beat oneself up with lofty levels of standards. It should be used to give yourself HONESTLY, with periodic check-ups to make sure you are going about things in your life correctly.

Another transparent moment to share: In my early adult life, I was very good at personal accountability, but it was tainted with a dose of pride. Here is what I mean. I often examined my actions, and it would seem to me that I was doing a terrific job, despite how others responded. Even if my actions caused an issue, I tend to believe that it had to be the other person's fault because I ALWAYS reminded me of ten things I know I did right before analyzing my wrongdoing. The good always blurred out bad. No one can grow from examining themselves through rose-colored lenses. I had to learn, and I believe I am still learning that still learn that I must examine myself with a lens of truth. We have to We must be honest with ourselves to grow and mature. We can't move forward just for the sake of moving forward. We should want to move for a reason of purpose. The goal is meaningful living and no longer existing.

Chapter 7

Supernatural Time Redemption

Why do we tend to say, "Man if I just had more time?" Or here's a common one; "Lord, please redeem the time that I wasted!" The questions we should immediately ask ourselves are, "What am I going to do with the redeemed time? Will I continue to spin my wheels and waste even more time? Am I going to do the same things day after day and expect change?" People, we MUST have some plan or idea about how we operate within the time we are given. Too often (I believe) we take for granted that assume we have all the time in the world, especially when we are young. When I was younger and heard the term, "Tomorrow is not promised," I did not believe that. I took for granted that assumed I would wake up the next day, then the next and the next.

We have to We must strive to maximize every moment of the day. You noticed that I did not say within a week or month or year. Those of us that tend to waste time and want redemption to have to redemption must take baby steps toward positioning ourselves to not waste the redemption of vapor. Stop and think before you start your day. Ask the Lord to help you formulate a good habit, better yet, a GOD habit today that will position you to maximize your moments. Only God can show you that. It is not a formula, but it is all about your relationship with Jesus Christ.

Ok, now that you are in position (I am speaking those things…YES GOD) to operate in your redeemed time; let's examine how to recognize the Hand of God during the redeemed time. One might think it is only measured or realized by the STUFF we supernaturally obtain, or even by divine favor. No, no, no! I believe we see supernatural time redemption through Godly influence. Things you have said over and over repeatedly to encourage people is heard by that appointed person that God placed in your path that has "influence." Your circumstance did not change; you did not suddenly get smarter, your words were the same. God just intervened and propelled you forward supernaturally!

Time for another transparent/personal moment. I almost did not share this testimony because it bares my soul. However, here it goes. I started preaching preached the Gospel at the age of 23. As a young man, I always wanted to be an amazing preacher and pastor. However, I doubted myself because I did not sound like my spiritual father or any of the well-known preachers I knew. I had a sincere desire to learn and to sharpen the spiritual gifts God gave me. I would sit in services of great prophets that would come to town and study them as they ministered, especially when they prayed and prophesied. I wanted so bad for the Lord to use me like that. I remember getting a chance to give my church a prophetic Word during a Sunday morning service. I was so nervous and the Word I gave (I believe God), but it was like no one responded, and my pastor shunned the utterance as if it was insignificant. I felt like hiding under a rock. I remember telling my wife that I would NEVER do that again.

Years past and we both went through times of healing within various churches. At the same time, simultaneously gathering some valuable training and teaching. Well, let me fast forward to now. God gave us the charge to launch a church in 2010, and in the past seven years, my wife and I have ministered to hundreds upon hundreds of people, and I sometimes wondered how this was going to happening. I had the same gifting I had when I was 18 years old. I have the same yearning to pastor that I had years ago. The difference (I know), is divine redemption clothed in Godly influence and timing! I do not know where my journey will end, but this one thing I do know who will be holding my hand and who holds my TIME! Our

Father God – the I AM that I AM! Joel 2:25 declares, *"And I will restore to you the years that the locust hath eaten, the cankerworm, and the caterpillar, and the palmerworm, my great army which I sent among you."* God has the power to redeem and restore to us the time we have wasted and the time the enemy has tricked us into forfeiting.

Listen, beloved, our pain, regrets, and sorrows over past failure, unfulfilled expectations, or tragedy can paralyze or destroy our ability to dream. We find ourselves locked in a prison of grief and regret without any hope for tomorrow.

Psalms 31: 14-15 declares: *"But as for me, I trust in You, O Lord; I say, You are my God! My times are in Your Hand…"* I challenge all of those that will read this book to allow God to manage your time. I promise He will do a better job of it than we can. The fact that that you are still alive qualifies you for time redemption. We are all on assignment. How do I know, we are still here! It is not too late to write that song, start that business, go back to school, etc. The very thing that seems impossible just might be the very thing that will propel you into destiny!

God wants you to be set free to dream again, not only to dream your dream but to dream a God-sized and God-inspired dream–a divine daring dream. God wants to release you from the prison of doubt, grief, and shame to be free to dream again where you can dream again–to imagine the divine daring dream– God will empower you to overcome barriers that held you back. God doesn't just want you to be a dreamer; God wants to see all your dreams come true.

Prayer: Father, I thank You for my life, dreams and passions. I praise You for the double portion, financial breakthroughs, restorations, miracles and deliverances for me, my family and everyone connected to me. I will be what You have already called me to be, in Jesus name.

Biography

Pastor Alvin M. Rucker is from Hartwell, GA. He is an honor graduate of Hart County High school. Pastor Rucker also holds a B.A. in Psychology from Morehouse College in Atlanta, GA. He is currently the senior pastor of One Accord Family Ministries in Pascagoula, MS. He has 17 years of experience as a mortgage loan officer. He has been pastoring for seven years and in the ministry for over 22 years. He has traveled and ministered in Georgia, Alabama, Mississippi, Louisiana, and Maryland. He is the husband of Pastor Kelli L. Rucker, and they have one son, Dylan Rucker. They currently reside in Moss Point, MS.

www.ingramcontent.com/pod-product-compliance
Lightning Source LLC
LaVergne TN
LVHW051207080426
835508LV00021B/2849